VAMPIRE KNIGHT™

Story & Art by
Matsuri Hino

Vol. 3

VAMPIRE KNIGHT™

Contents

VAMPIRE KNIGHT

TENTH NIGHT: THE LORD OF THE MOON DORMITORY

The Story of VAMPIRE KNIGHT

1 Cross Academy, a private boarding school, is where the Day Class and the Night Class coexist. The Night Class—a group of beautiful, elite students—are all vampires!

2 Zero was bitten by a pureblood vampire! Unable to resist his vampire instincts, he sank his fangs into Yuki. Zero blamed himself and tried to leave the school, but Yuki stopped him.

3 The next time Zero lusted after Yuki's blood, the vampire hunter Yagari appeared. Zero was resigned to dying at the hand of his former master. Zero tried to give up on everything and accept his fate...so Yuki offered her blood to him!!

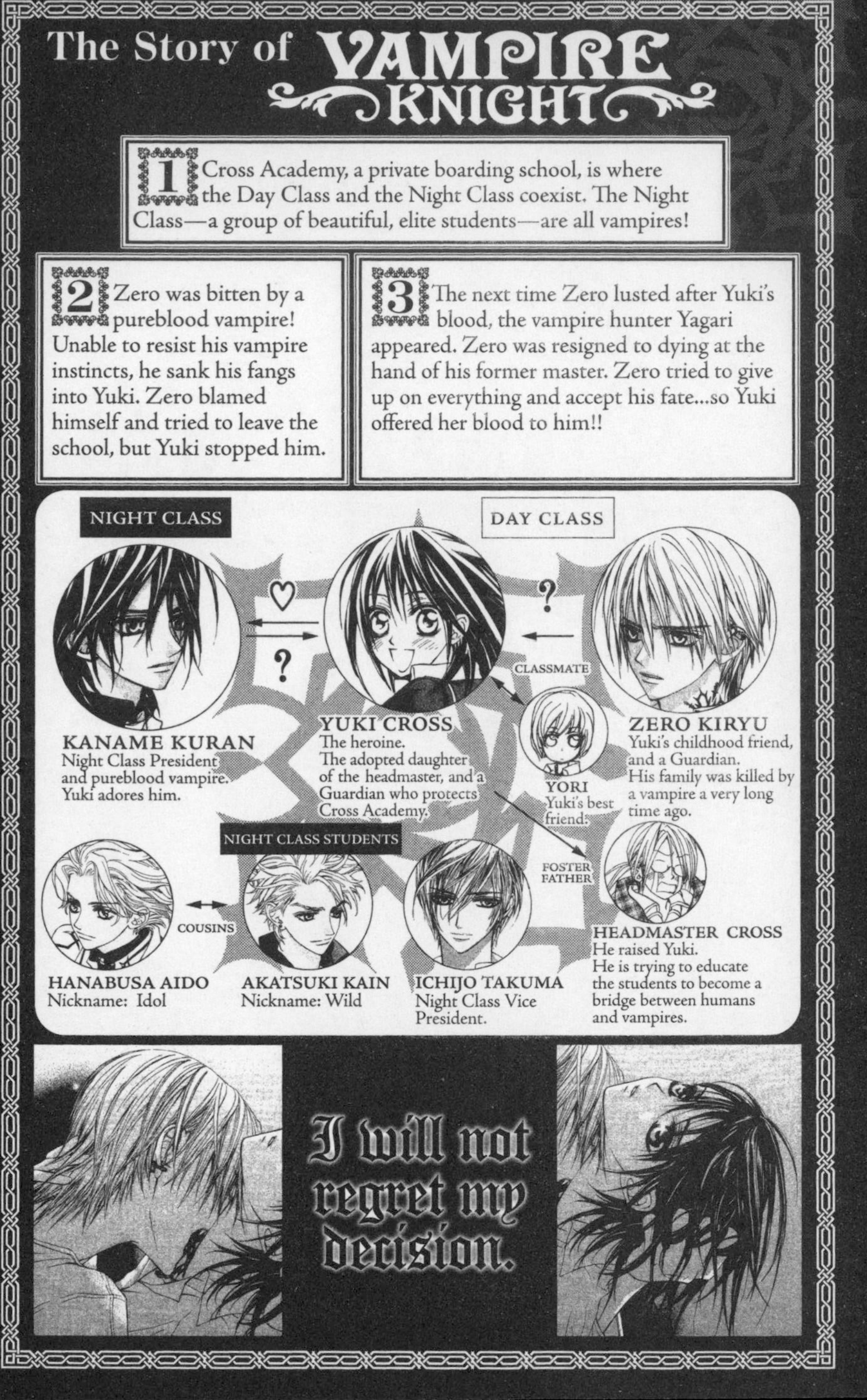
NIGHT CLASS
DAY CLASS
?
?
CLASSMATE
KANAME KURAN
Night Class President and pureblood vampire. Yuki adores him.
YUKI CROSS
The heroine.
The adopted daughter of the headmaster, and a Guardian who protects Cross Academy.
YORI
Yuki's best friend.
ZERO KIRYU
Yuki's childhood friend, and a Guardian.
His family was killed by a vampire a very long time ago.
NIGHT CLASS STUDENTS
FOSTER FATHER
COUSINS
HANABUSA AIDO
Nickname: Idol
AKATSUKI KAIN
Nickname: Wild
ICHIJO TAKUMA
Night Class Vice President.
HEADMASTER CROSS
He raised Yuki.
He is trying to educate the students to become a bridge between humans and vampires.
I will not regret my decision.

SHUP
SHFF
TMP

MORN-ING!
HEY.
CROSS ACADEMY, MOON DORMITORY
KNOCK KNOCK
KANAME.
...

SUFF
KNOWING YOU, YOU MUST HAVE SOMETHING ON YOUR MIND AGAIN.
MAKE SURE YOU GET SOME REST.
SLEEP WELL...

IT'S NOT UNUSUAL FOR KANAME TO WANT TO BE ALONE.
HOWEVER, I CAN TELL THAT SOMETHING HAPPENED LAST NIGHT...
...BUT IF I PRESS HIM, I'M AFRAID OF WHAT WILL HAPPEN TO ME AFTER-WARDS.
MORE-OVER, HE WOULDN'T WANT ME TO PRY.
OH, ICHIJO-SAMA.
YOU HAVEN'T GONE TO BED YET.
THE BOOKS YOU ORDERED ARE ALL HERE. SHALL I TAKE THEM TO YOUR ROOM?
OH...
UM.
YES, PLEASE.
I'LL JUST TAKE THIS MAGAZINE WITH ME NOW.
WHERE'S KURAN-SAMA?
YOU NEED TO TALK TO THE DORM PRESIDENT?

YES...
A GUEST WHO WILL BE VISITING THE DORM IS REQUESTING PERMISSION TO ENTER...
IT'S URGENT...
I, TAKUMA ICHIJO, AM VICE PRESIDENT OF THE NIGHT CLASS AND THE MOON DORMITORY...
KANAME IS BUSY RIGHT NOW...
...SO I'LL SIGN FOR HIM.
YES.
...BUT I REALIZE I'M USEFUL ONLY AT TIMES LIKE THIS.
UH?
FLUP
NO...
...WHY IS HE BOTHERING TO VISIT HERE?
TRMBL
TRMBL
TRMBL
HE'S COMING HERE. DO YOU WANT TO CONFIRM IT BY PHONE?
SUP

OH!
VOOM
TMP TMP TMP TMP
TMP TMP TMP TMP
BAM
WAKE UP! TONIGHT MY GRANDFATHER WILL BE HERE!
HUFF HUFF
ZAA
ZAA
...
...
ICHIJO, ARE YOU REALLY A VAMPIRE?
WHY DO YOU HAVE SO MUCH ENERGY DURING THE DAY?
VUUNK

WHY DON'T YOU GO PLAY IN THE SUNLIGHT AND TURN TO DUST...
SLEEPY
...JUST LIKE THE VAMPIRE IN THE MANGA YOU FORCED ME TO READ...
SHFF
I WOULD TURN TO DUST IF I COULD...
BUT IT'S BARELY LIGHT OUT...
IT'S BRIGHT!!
I'M GONNA KILL YOU!
GL
OMP
WHAT'S WITH THIS GUY...
YOU'RE REALLY AFRAID OF YOUR GRANDFATHER, AREN'T YOU, VICE PRESIDENT? HE'S THAT VAMPIRE...
JO
LT
DOOOM
YES.

I

Hello!! Thank you for reading!

It's the third volume...it snuck up on us. This time, because of the number of pages and time, I couldn't draw too many bonus manga. To the people who were looking forward to them, I'm sorry. I'm glad there are people who look forward to the extras. I've got to do my best with the main story too...

I consulted with my editor about the cover illustration for this volume--it's the first cover without the main characters. I'm curious to know what everyone thinks about it. The illustration of Yuki and Zero on the back cover was the cover illustration for the *La La* October 2005 issue. The designer requested that the two wear the white uniforms. It's my third favorite illustration from *Vampire Knight*.

IN THE HUMAN WORLD, HE MADE THE ICHIJO GROUP GROW SO LARGE THAT NOW ALL HUMAN BUSINESS TRANSACTIONS INVOLVE HIS COMPANY.
IN THE VAMPIRE WORLD, HE'S THE HEAD OF THE MOST DISTINGUISHED CLAN OF ARISTOCRATS.
ASATO ICHIJO... ALSO KNOWN AS ICHIO.
ONE OF THE OLDEST VAMPIRES ON THE SENATE...
WE HAVE NOTHING TO FEAR.
THE SENATE IS INDEED THE HIGHEST GOVERNING BODY OF OUR WORLD...
...BUT THEY ARE NOT OUR SOVEREIGN.
YES... WELL THAT IS TRUE, BUT...

I DON'T WANT THE RELATIVE PEACE IN THIS DORM DISTURBED TOO MUCH...
...FOR KANAME'S SAKE TOO.
TAK
TAK
...

HMPH. EVEN YOU GUYS ARE HERE AS LOYAL GREETERS.
ARE YOU THAT AFRAID OF THE OLD GEEZER IN THE SENATE?
OF COURSE...
HE'S A MONSTER WHO'S BEEN ALIVE TWELVE TIMES LONGER THAN WE HAVE.
THAT'S WHY EVERYONE CUT CLASSES TO BE HERE, RIGHT?
HE ADMITS IT...
I'M AFRAID TOO, RIMA.
BUT...
...WHO'S MORE SCARY, HIM OR PRESIDENT KURAN, THE PUREBLOOD?
YOU DON'T EVEN NEED TO ASK.

KANAME!
IT'S ALL RIGHT. YOU DON'T NEED TO BE HERE.
HE'S PROBABLY JUST COMING HERE TO LECTURE ME.
I WANT TO SAY HELLO TO ICHIO SINCE I HAVEN'T SEEN HIM FOR SO LONG.
MAY I?
OF COURSE YOU MAY...

OH
CHINK
BAM
HYOO
TAK

KREEE
TAK
WELL, WELL...
A VAMPIRE WHO HAS LIVED FOR A LONG, LONG TIME...
FOR THOSE WHO FACE HIM, HIS GAZE AND HIS BREATH...
I DEEPLY APPRECIATE ALL YOU COMING TO GREET ME...
...BUT I CAME ONLY TO VISIT MY DARLING GRANDSON.
YOU DON'T HAVE TO STAND ON FORMALITIES.

...ARE LIKE POISON.
ICHIO...
...I'M GLAD YOU SEEM TO BE IN EXCELLENT HEALTH.
WE HAVEN'T SEEN EACH OTHER SINCE THE DAY YOU REFUSED TO HAVE ME AS YOUR LEGAL GUARDIAN...
... KANAME-SAMA.
I DIDN'T WANT TO BE CODDLED.
KANAME... NOT HERE...

YOU'RE RIGHT.
TAK
KANAME-SAMA...
...PURE-BLOODS ARE DIFFERENT FROM ARISTO-CRATS...
...EVEN IF YOU'RE COVERED IN BLOOD, NOTHING CAN DEFILE YOU...
...YOU'RE A FLOWER THAT SMELLS LUSCIOUSLY SWEET FOR ETERNITY...

YOUR OVER-WHELMING YOUTH, POWER, BEAUTY...
...I PRAY THAT SOMEDAY...
...I WILL BE ABLE TO RECEIVE THE BENEFITS OF YOUR UNRIVALLED BLOOD...
KANAME-SAMA!

I'M SORRY, KANAME-SAMA...
...BUT...
THE DAUGHTER OF SOUEN AND THE SON OF AIDO...
YOU JEST TOO MUCH, SIR.
STOP IT, RUKA.
LET GO.
AIDO.
YOU SAY THAT, KNOWING THAT ASKING A PUREBLOOD FOR HIS BLOOD IS THE GREATEST TABOO AMONG VAMPIRES!

I'M NOT AFRAID OF YOU...
SLAP
...
I HAVEN'T TAUGHT HIM ENOUGH MANNERS.
BECAUSE YOU ARE HERE, KANAME-SAMA...
...I FEEL AT EASE KEEPING MY GRANDSON IN THIS ACADEMY...

...MY
LORD...

RUKA...
...IF I CONTINUE TO IGNORE YOU, WILL YOU STAND THERE FOREVER?
CHAK
KANAME-SAMA...
TMP
YOU HAVEN'T REPRI-MANDED ME YET...
HEH
YOU WANT ME TO SLAP YOU?
YOU'RE A STRANGE GIRL...
YOU'RE A KIND PERSON, KANAME-SAMA...

YOU RESCUED AIDO FROM ICHIO, DIDN'T YOU?
IT JUST TURNED OUT THAT WAY.
RECENTLY...
...YOU HAVEN'T BEEN YOUR USUAL SELF...
SHFF
I'M FINE.
KANAME-SAMA...

IF MY BLOOD CAN BE SUSTENANCE FOR YOU, EVEN A LITTLE...
PRIK
PLIP
VOLT
SUEE
...AND...
THAT'S ENOUGH, RUKA...
SUP
...THERE'S NOTHING TO WORRY ABOUT. I'M FINE.

ALL RIGHT.
WHAT?
NOTHING.
WHAT IS IT?
YO.
YOU KNOW...
...KANAME-SAMA WOULDN'T DRINK MY BLOOD.
BLUSH
I YEARNED FOR HIM...
...BUT HE REFUSED.
WHEN I FIRST CAME TO THIS SCHOOL, KANAME-SAMA DRANK MY BLOOD...
...BUT ONLY THAT ONE TIME...
YEAH.

WE VAMPIRES...
...TRY TO FULFILL OUR LONGINGS BY DRINKING ANOTHER VAMPIRE'S BLOOD.
IT MEANS THAT YOUR BLOOD IS NOT ENOUGH FOR HIM NOW.
I LOVE HIM SO MUCH...
I'M A FOOL...
...I'VE NEVER REALLY UNDERSTOOD KANAME-SAMA...
TAKUMA.

YES, GRAND-FATHER...
SERVE HIM WELL...
...AND KEEP AN EYE ON HIM.
KANAME-SAMA SEEMS TO TRUST YOU VERY MUCH...
THIS IS WHY I'M LETTING YOU ATTEND THIS ACADEMY.
KREEE
GRAND-FATHER...
...YOU DON'T UNDER-STAND.

I WILL NOT DO ANYTHING THAT GOES AGAINST MY FRIEND'S BEST INTERESTS.
UH...
D-DON'T GLARE AT ME...
YOU'RE THE ONE WHO DOESN'T UNDER-STAND.
A FRIENDSHIP BASED ON A FICTITIOUS PEACE...
...IN THE SMALL WORLD OF THIS ACADEMY--

UM...
S-SO THE HEADMASTER SAID HE WANTS YOU TO DONATE A LOT THIS TIME TOO.
YOU ARE ICHIJO'S GRAND-FATHER, RIGHT?
CROSS ACADEMY IS TRULY PEACEFUL!
I WOULD LOVE TO HEAR WHY THE HEADMASTER CONSIDERS THIS PLACE PEACEFUL.
I EVEN HEARD THAT A COMMISSIONED VAMPIRE HUNTER ENTERED THE ACADEMY GROUNDS THE OTHER DAY.
GEH
YUKI?!

I WAS TOLD BY THE HEADMASTER TO BRING YOU TO HIM IMMEDIATELY.
THE HEADMASTER WOULD LIKE TO EXPLAIN THAT MATTER AS WELL.
ZERO?
ZERO...
...YOU'RE FEELING BETTER?
CROSS... HE'S AS IMPUDENT AS EVER...

ALL RIGHT.
SHOW ME THE WAY.
ZERO! I'LL GO WITH YOU!
WAIT, YUKI!

DID SOMETHING HAPPEN BETWEEN YOU AND KANAME?
...WHY ARE YOU ASKING ME THAT?
... NO...
WELL...
...KANAME DOESN'T TELL ME THE IMPORTANT THINGS...
...SO I THOUGHT YOU MIGHT KNOW SOME-THING, YUKI.
UM...
...I DIDN'T EVEN KNOW KANAME WAS A PUREBLOOD.
I REALLY DON'T KNOW ANYTHING...

BUT...
...YOU USED TO BE VERY CLOSE.
YOU...
...KNOW A SIDE OF KANAME THAT WE'VE NEVER SEEN.
KANAME-SAMA!
TENTH NIGHT/END

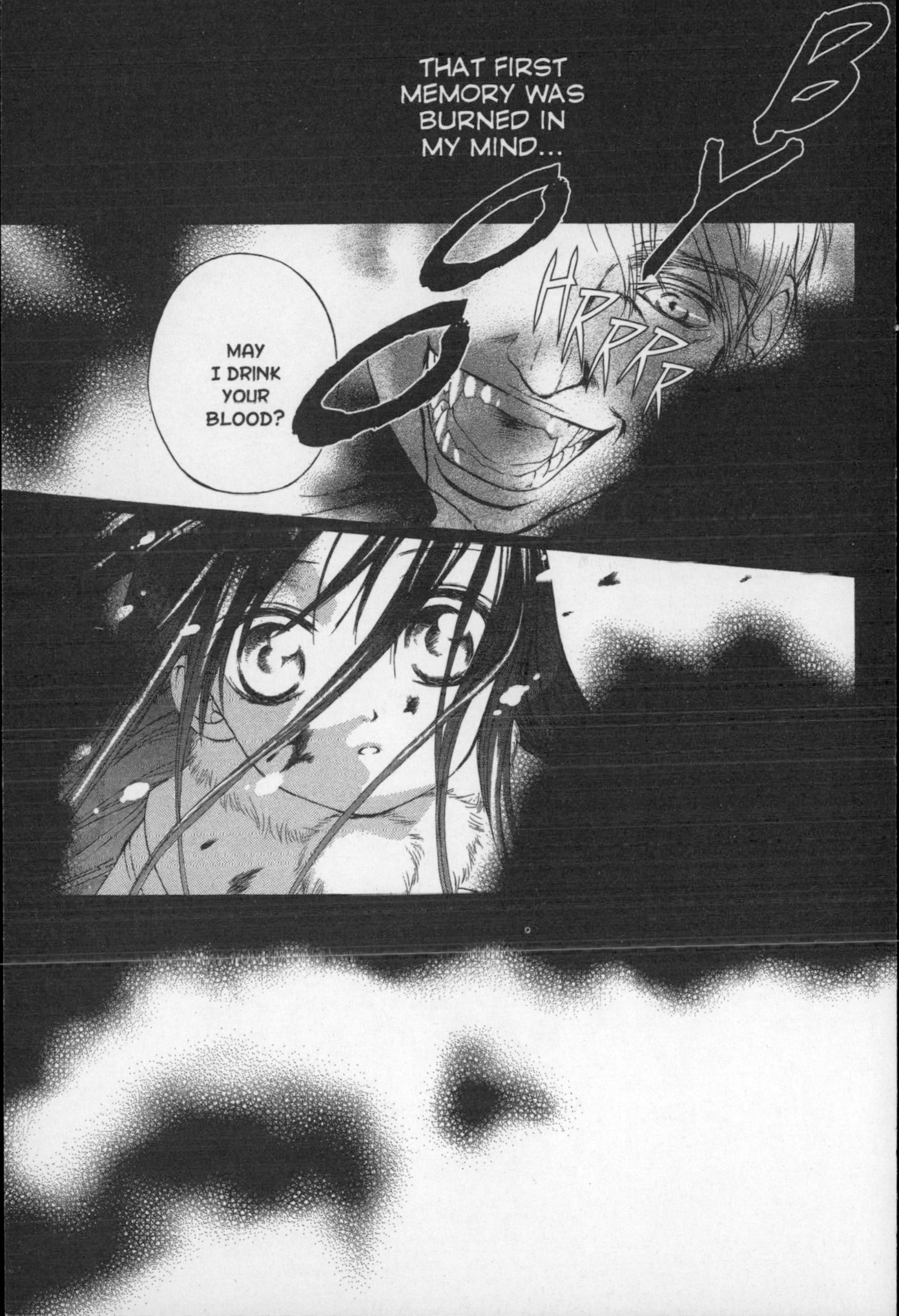
THAT FIRST MEMORY WAS BURNED IN MY MIND...
HRRRR
MAY I DRINK YOUR BLOOD?

THE SECOND MEMORY...
ARE YOU ALL RIGHT?
VAMPIRE KNIGHT
ELEVENTH NIGHT: MEMORIES OF SNOW, BLOOD, AND TENDERNESS

SUFF
SNIFF
DON'T.
HEY.
WHY ARE YOU OUT HERE ALONE?

COME WITH ME.
I'M KANAME.
WHAT'S YOUR NAME?
...
TRMBL
TRMBL
MY EARLIEST MEMORY IS OF THAT SNOWY DAY TEN YEARS AGO.

WHITE SNOW, RED BLOOD...
...TERROR...
...YOU WERE SCARED.
IT'S ALL RIGHT NOW.
OF COURSE...
HUH...
UH...
...AND THE MEMORY OF BEING HELD TENDERLY...
BLAM
BLAM

BLAM
BLAM
BLAM
BLAM
SHF
SHK
YOU DON'T COME TO THE SHOOTING RANGE OFTEN. IT'S ODD TO SEE YOU HERE.
WHAT ARE YOU LOOKING AT?

WHA...
WHAT?!
WHAT'S WITH THAT LOOK?
CAN'T I WATCH?
...
I'M WORRIED, ZERO... ABOUT WHETHER YOU'RE REALLY ALL RIGHT...
...I SHOULD BE LOOKING OUT FOR YOU.
BEING A CARE-TAKER...
...IS HARD WORK.
I'LL LOSE MY CONCEN-TRATION.
GRRR!!
THAT'S THE WAY HE TALKS TO ME! TYPICAL.
SO MEAN

BLAM
BLAM
BLAM
BLAM
BLAM
YOU'RE...
THERE'S...
...SUCH...
...DOING REALLY WELL.
...A BONE-CHILLING ATMOSPHERE...
BLAM
STOP WEARING THAT GAUZE AROUND YOUR NECK.
IT'S TOO OBVIOUS.
BUT I NEED IT.
IF I JUST PUT A BANDAGE ON IT, PEOPLE LIKE AIDO RIP IT OFF.

ACTUALLY, HE MIGHT ALREADY HAVE FIGURED IT OUT...
I SHOULD KEEP IT ON UNTIL YOUR FANG MARKS ARE LESS OBVIOUS.
...
IF YOU WERE GOING TO HAVE SOMEBODY DRINK YOUR BLOOD...
...I GUESS YOU WOULD HAVE WANTED...
...KANAME KURAN...
...TO DRINK IT...
WHAT?

I KNOW YOU LIKE KANAME KURAN.
I COULD TELL.
EVEN YOUR BLOOD...
...TASTED THAT WAY...
THAT SOUNDS... PERVERTED.
KLANK
I FEEL LIKE YOU'RE PEEKING INSIDE ME.
TMP

CHIK
BLAM
KANAME KURAN...
YOU USED TO BE VERY CLOSE.
I DON'T WANT PEOPLE TALKING ABOUT US!

I KNOW BEST...
...WHAT KANAME IS TO ME.
OF COURSE.
I'LL LOOK AFTER THIS CHILD, KANAME.
BWOING
BWOING
YOU'RE THE SURVIVING SON OF THE PERSON I OWE A LOT TO.
SNIFF SNIFF

SHE DOESN'T EVEN SEEM TO UNDERSTAND THAT THE PUDDING IS FOOD...
YES... SHE SEEMS TO HAVE LOST ALL HER MEMORIES...
...
POKE
SCOOP IT WITH A SPOON... THERE.
OPEN YOUR MOUTH.
JOLT
WHAT?
SAY "AHH..."
...

TUP
EEEEEEK!

HEAD-MASTER.
I THINK IT'S BETTER IF I LEAVE AND NEVER SEE HER AGAIN.
I'M GOING HOME.
GOING HOME? YOU MEAN TO THAT PLACE?
JUST WHEN YOU WERE FINALLY ABLE TO LEAVE...
THAT PLACE IS A DEN OF DEMONS...
...WHO WANT TO USE YOU SINCE YOUR PARENTS HAVE PASSED AWAY.
BUT... I CAN'T NOT GO BACK.
...
GOODBYE.

THAT PERSON SAID TO ME...
..."GIRLS ARE BORN PRINCESSES."
SO FROM TODAY, I'LL GIVE YOU A NAME THAT MEANS "TENDER PRINCESS"...
YOU'LL BE "YUKI." IS THAT OKAY?
EVEN LATER, NO ONE COULD DISCOVER WHO I WAS...
YUKI!
YOU WEAR THAT ON YOUR FOOT!
...SO I WAS LEGALLY ADOPTED BY THE HEADMASTER.
...
...
IT'S BEEN A WEEK AND YOU HAVEN'T SPOKEN A WORD.

CHAK
...
GOOD EVENING, KANAME.
WHAT BRINGS YOU HERE?
WHAT?
I RECEIVED AN EMAIL THAT A VAMPIRE CHASED THAT LITTLE GIRL AND ATTACKED THIS PLACE...
I SHOOK OFF MY GUARDS AND RUSHED OVER HERE... BUT I TAKE IT...
...YOU LIED.
KRSSSH
HEH HEH HEH

BLUSH
I'M NEVER GOING TO BELIEVE ANYTHING YOU SAY AGAIN.
KANAME! KANAME!
!
OH NO!
LOOK!
SHAKE
SHAKE
WHAT HAPPENED ?!
YUKI GOT DRESSED BY HERSELF!
ALTHOUGH SHE'S WEARING HER CLOTHES ALL WRONG.
OH
FUMP
...
...
BATH TOWEL

KLUTCH
WHAT?!
KANAME?
HUH?
HA...
AH HA HA HA HA HA...
AH...
HA HA HA HA...
BAM BAM
DITHER DITHER
WH-WHAT SHOULD I DO?! KANAME HAS GONE BERSERK!
HE'S LAUGHING? I DIDN'T KNOW HE HAD A SENSE OF HUMOR!
SORRY.
I...
I SHOULDN'T BE LAUGHING...
HA...
HA HA HA HA.
HAAH...
...
HEH
AH...

II

In volume 2 I said I'd fill these spaces by thinking up some "themes," so I'll try it out. This is something I've been doing to get a grip on the characters...

● Theme No. 1 "Who will survive when left in the middle of the jungle?" (Limited to guys only)

It has nothing to do with the story, does it? ♭ But I seriously thought about this. Depending on the situation, those who have a high probability of not being able to survive are Zero, Aido, and Kain. If Zero is alone, he might say, "I don't care..." and not try to survive. Aido would be grumbling--he'd yell at the ivy entangling him and would move forward, but I have doubts about whether he can procure food (because he's a pampered young man to the core).

(continues)
↓

I'M SORRY FOR SCARING YOU.
I'LL LEAVE YOU BE.
VUP
HA...
BYE-BYE.

A GENTLE AND TENDER TIME BEGAN...

KANAME-SAMA!
WHY "SAMA"?
TODAY IS YUKI'S BIRTHDAY!
IT'S "THE DAY KANAME-SAMA RESCUED YUKI A YEAR AGO"!
I SNUCK OUT AND RUSHED OVER BECAUSE I HEARD YUKI HAD BEEN KIDNAPPED.
CAN'T YOU ASK ME OVER HERE WITHOUT MAKING UP SOME-THING?
PWND
HUH? HEAD-MASTER?
AND WHY DID YOU TEACH HER TO CALL ME "SAMA"?!
HAPPY BIRTHDAY...
...KANAME-SAMA!
NO, YUKI.
RIGHT?
TODAY IS HAPPY BIRTHDAY TO YOU.

SLOWLY I BEGAN TO UNDERSTAND MANY THINGS.

KANAME-SAMA...
...IS A VAMPIRE, RIGHT?
YES.
THE GOVERNMENT HASN'T MADE IT PUBLIC THAT VAMPIRES EXIST...
...SO PLEASE KEEP IT A SECRET TOO, YUKI.
A SECRET...
IT'S A SECRET, BUT KANAME-SAMA LET ME TOUCH...
...HIS VAMPIRE FANGS.

KANAME-SAMA WON'T DO ANYTHING LIKE THAT SCARY VAMPIRE, RIGHT?
HE'S COMPLETELY DIFFERENT, RIGHT?
HAS KANAME EVER DONE ANYTHING THAT YOU DIDN'T WANT HIM TO, YUKI?
THERE ARE VAMPIRES YOU CAN BE FRIENDS WITH.
YES!
MY BIRTHDAY COMES ONCE A YEAR... IT WAS A SPECIAL DAY ON WHICH WE COULD MEET.
ONLY BRIEF MEETINGS WERE ALLOWED.

IF HE'S COMING TO VISIT US, HE SHOULD PASS BY HERE...
KANAME-SAMA...
...
B-BMP
B-BMP
WHY DO I FEEL SO ANXIOUS WALKING IN TOWN ALONE?
B-BMP
I'M ELEVEN YEARS OLD TODAY, SO I'VE GOT TO BE STRONGER...
B-BMP
I WAS TOLD A VAMPIRE WOULDN'T ATTACK ME IN TOWN.
B-BMP
KANAME-SAMA... YOU'RE STILL NOT HERE?
IT'S GETTING DARK...
B-BMP
BUT BE CAREFUL, YUKI...

...THERE ARE VAMPIRES WHO LIVE AMONG HUMANS IN TOWNS.
B-BMP
B-BMP

KUP
BOW

YUKI.
KANAME-SAMA!
WEREN'T YOU SCARED WALKING IN TOWN ALONE?
IF WE'RE TOGETHER, I'M NOT SCARED OF ANYTHING.

ME TOO.
KANAME-SAMA...
HOLD
THIS...

...HAPPENED WHEN I TRULY DIDN'T KNOW ANYTHING.
BUT THAT TIME CAME TO AN ABRUPT END.
BAM
YUKI!
I'M SORRY I'M LATE.

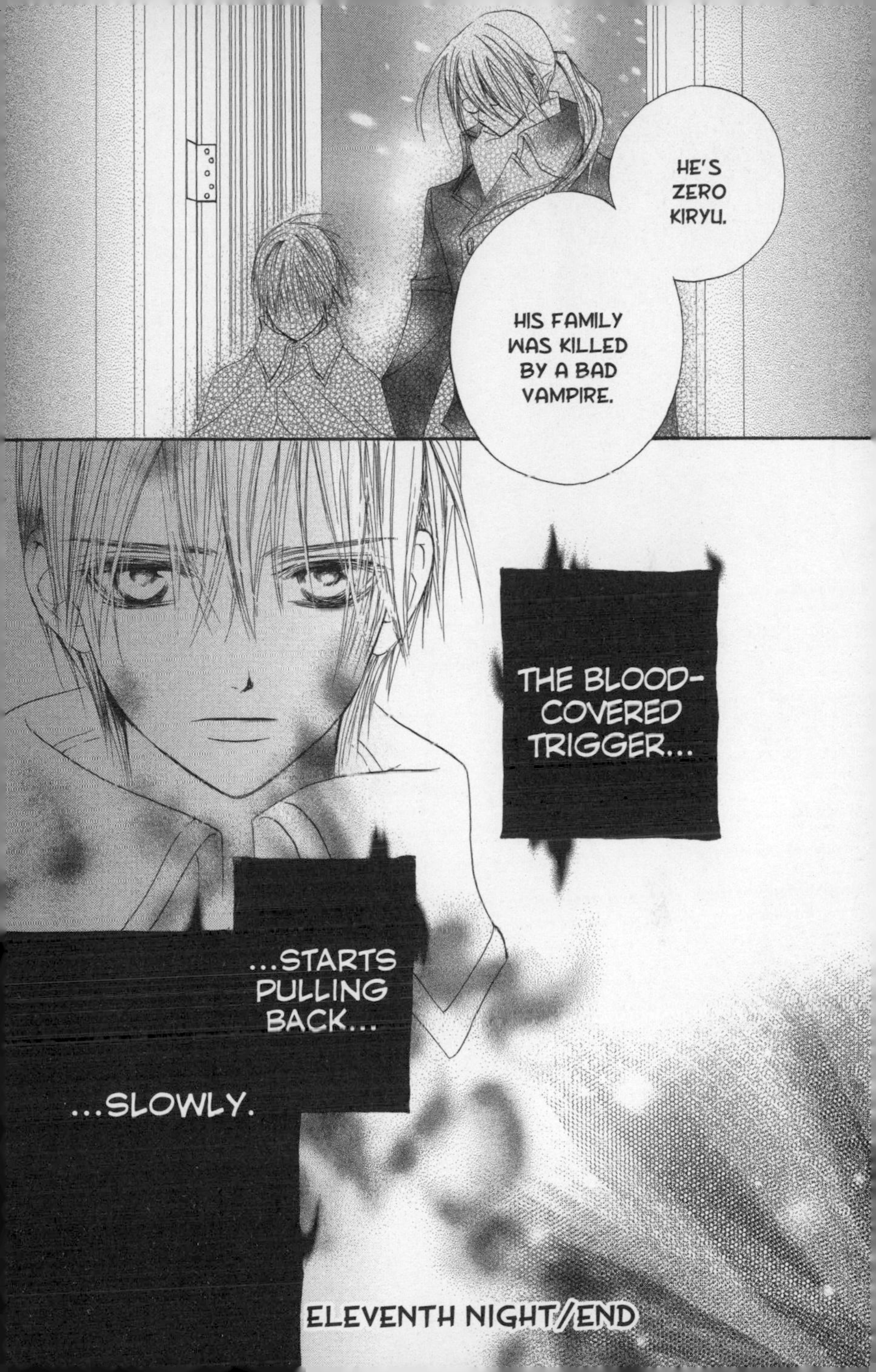
HE'S ZERO KIRYU.
HIS FAMILY WAS KILLED BY A BAD VAMPIRE.
THE BLOOD-COVERED TRIGGER...
...STARTS PULLING BACK...
...SLOWLY.
ELEVENTH NIGHT//END

VAMPIRE KNIGHT
TWELFTH NIGHT: WE WERE POWERLESS BACK THEN

VAMPIRES COVERED IN BLOOD ARE PROHIBITED FROM ENTERING THIS PAGE!!

✿ Kaname-sama is a Member of the Night Clan ✿

Yuki, it's late. Go to bed.
No!
Oh, Kaname.
Good evening.
Kaname-sama!
Listen! Yuki is refusing to go to bed!
If kids stay up late, it's very bad for their brain development...
...they said that on TV.
YOU WANT TO BECOME A STUPID GIRL, YUKI?
Was that really why?
Woo, flunked.

HEADMASTER'S BATHROOM
...
KNOCK
TOWEL
KIRYU IS IN THE BATH-ROOM.
WHY DON'T YOU USE THE ONE IN THE GUEST ROOM?
I'LL WAIT FOR HIM TO FINISH.
I NEED TO TALK TO HIM.
PLEASE FIX THE LOCK SOON.
TMPH

...I COULD TELL...
...EVEN YOUR BLOOD...
...TASTED THAT WAY...
ZERO...
...I DON'T WANT KANAME TO DRINK MY BLOOD...
NOT...
...EVER.
WHAT ARE VAMPIRES?
THEY CAN TELL WHO SOMEONE IS IN LOVE WITH BY DRINKING THEIR BLOOD?
YOU'RE WRONG, ZERO.
ALWAYS ...

...SINCE THAT TIME...
I...
...
WHAT ARE YOU DOING?
ZERO?
...
IT FEELS YUCKY...
...I CAN STILL FEEL THAT WOMAN HERE...

III

(continued)
↓
Kain could procure food easily, but he might keep wandering in the jungle. (It's not that I've made him to have no sense of direction, but somehow...)

On other hand, those who have a high probability of surviving are Kaname, Ichijo, and Shiki. And the Headmaster. Kaname would definitely survive, remaining silent and cool. Surviving isn't a big deal for him.

Ichijo would make a noisy fuss. But no matter how dire the situation gets, he'd be enjoying it quite a bit, and he'd succeed in escaping.

Shiki, with his animal-like instincts, would act the same as usual. The Headmaster... I don't quite understand it and it's creepy, but he'd survive...

Zero, Aido, and Kaname, who managed to survive, might retaliate against me for thinking up things like this...♪

KRRSH
STOP IT...
THAT MUST HURT...
STOP ...
KRRSH
ZERO!
YOU'RE TALKING ABOUT THE VAMPIRE WHO DID HORRIBLE THINGS TO YOUR FAMILY, RIGHT?
SHE DID... HORRIBLE THINGS TO YOU TOO, ZERO.
IT MUST HAVE BEEN...
...TERRIBLY SCARY...
GRIP

IV
By the way, in the Japanese edition of volume 2, there were errors in the kanji for "Kaname" and "pureblood." I'm sorry.♪ They've been corrected in the second edition... Also, in the magazine sometimes, the Night Class's black shirt is white...♪ I'll try to draw my manuscripts more calmly, with time to spare...
After this series started, there was a time when my editor thought I was a weapons maniac... No, I don't even know the formal name of the gun that I modeled Zero's gun after. (I just know that you see it often, and that it's a slightly older model...♪♪) I think I'm a tools maniac. Simply made, functioning tools are beautiful just to look at.

YOU'RE ALL RIGHT NOW...
...YOU'RE ALL RIGHT...
...I'LL BE WITH YOU ALWAYS...
...SO YOU'LL BE ALL RIGHT.

THE THREE OF US STARTED LIVING AT CROSS ACADEMY AROUND THIS TIME.
KIRYU...
...WE HAVE A GUEST...
SO LATE AT NIGHT?
DING DONG
...
IT'S ALL RIGHT, YUKI. GO GET HIM.
STAND
TMP
TMP
TMP
KIRYU... WHEN YOU SEE...
...I THINK YOU'LL UNDER-STAND.
UNDER-STAND WHAT?
KANAME-SAMA!

KANAME-SAMA.
UM...
WHAT IS IT?

B-BMP

...
ZERO...
B-BMP
B-BMP
NO, ZERO...!

ZUK
VAMPIRE!
KANAME-SAMA!
YOU JUST RUN UP AND STAB ME...?
THAT'S RATHER CRUEL.

SHUT UP, VAMPIRE!
THAT WOMAN?
YOU SMELL THE SAME AS THAT WOMAN!
THEN YOU'RE ZERO KIRYU?
I'VE HEARD ABOUT YOU.
I'M SORRY ABOUT WHAT HAPPENED TO YOUR FAMILY.
SHUP
BUT...
...I HAVE NO INTENTION OF LETTING YOU KILL ME.
KLAK

KIRYU, HE'S NOT THE ONE WHO WARRANTS YOUR REVENGE.
KANAME-SAMA...
...YOU'RE BLEED-ING...
IT'S NOTHING. IT'LL HEAL SOON.
I'M A VAMPIRE.
AND...
...HE'S THE ONE WHO IS IN PAIN...

I'M SORRY.
...I SHOULD'VE TOLD YOU ABOUT HIM EARLIER...
ZERO...
...KANAME-SAMA LEFT.
ARE YOU ALL RIGHT...? ZERO?
REACH
SLAP
DON'T TOUCH ME...
...WITH THE HAND YOU USED TO TOUCH HIM!

KANAME-SAMA IS A KIND VAMPIRE...
...WHO RESCUED ME FROM A SCARY VAMPIRE.
THERE'S SOME-THING WRONG...
...WITH BOTH HEAD-MASTER CROSS...
...AND YOU.
CHAK
YOU'RE BACK, KANAME.
YOU'RE EARLY. YOUR ERRAND IS DONE?
YUNK
NO... I'LL COME AGAIN ANOTHER TIME.
HM? BUT...
...I DIDN'T THINK YOU'D COME BACK HURT.
THERE'S...
...BLOOD ON YOUR WRIST.

HERE.
MOIST TOWEL-ETTES.
SUP
LICK
I MET THE SURVIVOR OF THAT INCIDENT.
SO THE HEAD-MASTER IS TAKING CARE OF HIM.
WELL... THAT'S TO BE EXPECTED.
WHAT IS IT?
ARE YOU JEALOUS BECAUSE HE CAN ALWAYS BE WITH YUKI?
I DON'T HAVE TIME TO BE JEALOUS.
THINGS WILL GET BUSY SOON.
AND SHORTLY AFTER THAT...

...THE HEADMASTER MADE A STRANGE PROPOSAL.
AS YOU TWO KNOW, I'M THE PRESIDENT AND HEADMASTER OF CROSS ACADEMY.
I'M GOING TO ESTABLISH A NIGHT CLASS AT OUR SCHOOL...
...STARTING NEXT YEAR!
NIGHT CLASS? DO YOU MEAN AN EVENING CLASS FOR THE SENIORS?
NO.
THE NIGHT CLASS IS THE NIGHT CLASS.
?
THEY'LL USE THE HIGH SCHOOL BUILDING AT NIGHT...
...BUT IT'S NOT FOR SENIORS OR COLLEGE STUDENTS.
WHAT ARE THE STUDENTS GOING TO DO AT NIGHT?
THEY'LL BE TAKING CLASSES, OF COURSE.
I'LL HAVE THEM DO ADVANCED STUDIES, AND THEY CAN ATTEND AS LONG AS THEY WANT.
BECAUSE ...

...THE STUDENTS ARE NOC-TURNAL...
...AND LIVE MUCH LONGER THAN WE DO...
...SO WE CAN'T DEAL WITH THEM LIKE WE DEAL WITH HUMANS.
THOK
EVERY STUDENT IN THE NIGHT CLASS...
...WILL BE...
...A VAMPIRE.
WHAT ARE YOU TRYING TO DO...
...LETTING THOSE THINGS IN THE SCHOOL?
HEAD-MASTER?

THE OBJECTIVE IS TO PROMOTE PEACEFUL COEXISTENCE BETWEEN VAMPIRES AND HUMANS...
...AND TO EDUCATE YOUNG VAMPIRES...
...SO THEY BECOME A POLITICALLY MODERATE FORCE.
KANAME, YOU CAME.
KANAME-SAMA?!
I DIDN'T KNOCK... BUT GOOD EVENING...
...YUKI.
KANAME KURAN... ?
...

DASH
IT'S RIDICULOUS!
THERE'S NO WAY VAMPIRES WOULD WANT TO COEXIST WITH HUMANS!
HOW MANY TIMES HAVE THEY SHED OUR BLOOD--
I WANT TO END ALL THAT.
I'VE LOST SOME-ONE TOO...
...JUST LIKE YOU, KIRYU.
...
THAT DOESN'T MEAN YOU HAVE THE RIGHT TO INVITE BEASTS INTO A HERD OF SHEEP!
ZERO DOESN'T AGREE, BUT YOU'VE ALREADY MADE UP YOUR MIND, HEAD-MASTER?

THERE'S NOTHING FOR YOU TWO TO WORRY ABOUT.
KURAN WILL ATTEND THE NIGHT CLASS...
...SO THE OTHER VAMPIRES WILL BEHAVE THEM-SELVES.
AND BECAUSE OF HIM, WE'RE GETTING OTHER STUDENTS TO ATTEND TOO.
...
BUT...
...THINGS ARE OVER IF HE DOUBLE-CROSSES US.
ZERO...
UM...
I'LL GO CHECK ON HIM.
TMP

KANAME...
I'M GLAD YOU SUPPORT MY PACIFISM.
TRULY.
YES, I HOPE YOUR IDEALS WILL BECOME REALITY.
AND SINCE MY ACTIONS ARE RE-STRICTED...
...I WANT STUDENTS WHO CAN MOVE AT MY BECK AND CALL.
THERE IS ONE THING...
...THAT WORRIES ME...
...BUT PLEASE DON'T BE CONCERNED.
I WILL ACT AS QUEEN BEE.

THE HEADMASTER WENT AHEAD WITH HIS PLANS THE FOLLOWING YEAR.
THAT'S THE OLD BUILDING WHERE THE TEACHERS USED TO LIVE... NO ONE IS LIVING THERE NOW, RIGHT?
IT'S A TEMPORARY DORM FOR THE NIGHT CLASS UNTIL THEY'RE DONE WITH THEIR ENTRANCE EXAMS OR THEIR VOWS OR SOMETHING.
THE VAMPIRES ARE THERE.
DON'T GET TOO CLOSE...
...TO THEIR LAIR.
THEN...
...KANAME-SAMA IS LIVING THERE NOW TOO...

KREE
TMP
OH? IT'S YUKI.
YOU CAME TO SEE KANAME?
EEK!
I'M SORRY.
KANAME IS OUT RIGHT NOW.
HE'S NOT OUT PARTYING, BY THE WAY. ♡
WHAT?
HUH? UM...
YOU...
...KNOW WHO I AM?
YES.
I USED TO LIVE WITH KANAME... WE DROVE TO YOUR PLACE OFTEN.
HE SAW...
HE'S VERY FRIENDLY...
...BUT HE'S A VAMPIRE TOO.
I STAYED INSIDE THE CAR, BUT I ALWAYS WATCHED YOU HUGGING KANAME TIGHTLY♡, YUKI.
FROM FAR AWAY.
OKAY, YUKI! YOU SHOULD GO HOME AND GET TO BED.
YOU SHOULDN'T BE OUT AT NIGHT, EVEN ON THE SCHOOL GROUNDS!
HE TOLD ME TO GO HOME, BUT...

KREEE
IT'S COLD IN HERE...
...I'LL WAIT FOR KANAME-SAMA INSIDE...
HE'S SO CLOSE... JUST A LITTLE BIT FARTHER...
SUMP
THERE'S A THOUSAND QUESTIONS ON THIS SURVEY!
!
HEADMASTER CROSS MUST BE TWISTED. WE HAVE TO FILL THIS OUT TONIGHT.
THAT'S BECAUSE YOU'RE TRYING TO ANSWER THE QUESTIONS SERIOUSLY.
I JUST SCRIB-BLED STUFF DOWN.
A VAMPIRE TRYING TO EARNESTLY ANSWER A SURVEY...
HEE
...THAT'S FUNNY...
...
JOLT
BOW

SIGH
SU
FF

YOU'RE LYING IN HARM'S WAY...
SHUP
SHUFF

TOK
TOK
YOU DON'T KNOW THE RULES OF THE NIGHT CLASS YET?
SORRY...
...I JUST REMEMBERED.
I'LL GO BACK TO MY ROOM AND FINISH THE SURVEY.

UH...
SHE'S LOOKING THIS WAY... IS SHE A FAN OF MINE?
SHE'S LAUGHING AT YOU.
WHY IS THERE A HUMAN CHILD HERE?
DON'T CAUSE PROBLEMS BEFORE SCHOOL EVEN STARTS, ALL RIGHT?
I DON'T WANT MY SCHOOL LIFE WITH KANAME-SAMA TO BE SPOILED BY FOOLISH THINGS.
I'M NOT THAT STUPID.
YOU'RE BEING RUDE.
THEY'RE ALL BEAUTIFUL.
SHE CALLED HIM "KANAME-SAMA"...
...SHE LIKES KANAME-SAMA TOO...
TOK
TOK
WHAT SHOULD I DO? WILL THE HEADMASTER NOTICE I'M NOT IN BED?
KANAME-SAMA...
...IF ALL VAMPIRES WERE LIKE THE STUDENTS HERE...
...WE ALL COULD TRULY COEXIST...

IN MY
DREAM...

...I FELT SOMEONE WHISPERING...
...THAT I WAS BEING CRUEL.
SHIFF
HM?
WHERE...
...AM I?
...
THIS...
...IS KANAME-SAMA'S COAT...

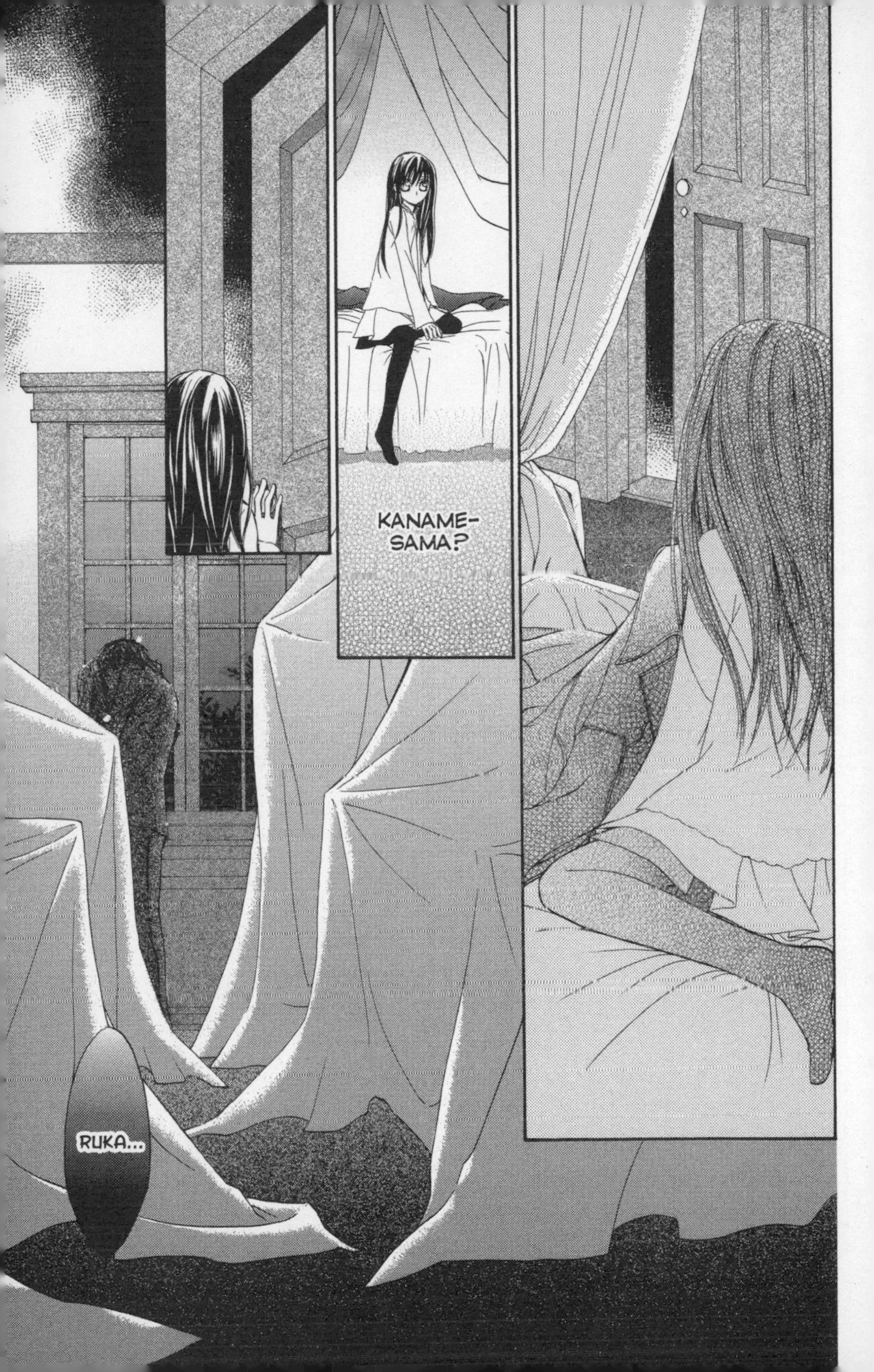
KANAME-SAMA?
RUKA...

AH...
PNNT
KANA...
...SA...
RIIV
NO MORE ...
...

KREE
YES...
IT'S BEST TO RUN AWAY.
SUFF

YUKI...
...YOU MAKE ME CRUEL...
KREEEE
B-BMP
B-BMP
KANAME-SAMA!
AH!
TUMP
HUFF
HUFF
KANAME-SAMA...
WHY?
JOLT

ZERO...
...
THE HEAD-MASTER...
...TOLD ME TO COME GET YOU.
DID KANAME KURAN...
...DO SOME-THING TO YOU?
VIP VIP
UNBELIEVABLE!
I CAN SMELL BLOOD EVERY-WHERE!
VAMPIRES...
ARE THEY TAUNTING US?
!

OH...
LET'S GET GOING.
YOU SHOULD TELL THE HEAD-MASTER WHAT HAPPENED AND CLEAN YOUR WOUND.
GRIP
VAMPIRES...
B-BMP
B-BMP
...
THEY LUST FOR BLOOD. THEY DEVOUR.

AND SOMETIMES...
THEY DON'T HESITATE TO KILL.
THEY'RE BEASTS IN HUMAN FORM...
...JUST LIKE KANAME KURAN.
YOU KNEW THAT ALREADY, RIGHT?
BUT...
...KANAME-SAMA SAVED MY LIFE.

I'M ALIVE NOW BECAUSE OF KANAME-SAMA.
KANAME-SAMA IS DIFFERENT...
THEN...
...STOP TREMBLING. IT'S A DISGRACE.
THAT NIGHT, I STARTED TO FEAR VAMPIRES ONCE AGAIN...

SOMETHING CHANGED INSIDE ME FROM THAT TIME ON.
THE NIGHT CLASS IS MOVING INTO THE MOON DORM TODAY?
CAN I COME WITH YOU, HEAD-MASTER?
PRESI-DENT KURAN.
...LET'S GO.
YES...
KANAME-SAMA IS DIFFERENT FROM ME.
THANK YOU FOR CARRYING ME THE OTHER DAY...
KANAME-SAMA...

BUT THERE WAS SOME-THING THAT DID NOT CHANGE.
EVEN IF KANAME-SAMA IS DIFFERENT, I STILL LOVE HIM...
KREE

ARE YOU ASLEEP?
YOU'LL CATCH A COLD...
HEY.
WAKE...
MM?
KANAME-SAMA...

B-BMP
B-BMP
SLUMP
B-BMP

B-BMP
...
B-BMP

OH
DON'T BE ALARMED. I'M JUST HERE TO TALK TO THE HEAD-MASTER.
I USED TO COME HERE OFTEN WITHOUT PRIOR NOTICE.
BY THE WAY...
...I'VE NEVER TOLD YOU...
...WHY I'M PRETENDING NOT TO NOTICE WHAT HAS HAPPENED TO YOU.
...
I KNOW HOW PRECARIOUS THE PEACE IS HERE AT CROSS ACADEMY.
SO I THOUGHT ABOUT...
...WHO COULD ACT AS YUKI'S SHIELD IN THIS PLACE.

YOU WILL NOT DOUBLE-CROSS HER...
...BECAUSE YOU OWE HER THAT MUCH...
THAT IS WHY...
...I'M...
...ALLOWING YOU TO LIVE.
TWELFTH NIGHT/END

VAMPIRE KNIGHT

THIRTEENTH NIGHT: HE WHO PULLS THE TRIGGER

YOU CANNOT DOUBLE-CROSS HER...
...BECAUSE YOU OWE HER THAT MUCH...
THAT IS WHY I'M...
...ALLOWING YOU TO LIVE.
GRIP
KANAME KURAN...
...HAS NOTHING TO DO WITH IT...

CHAK
PHOO! I'M TIRED!
OH, ZERO.
WERE YOU ABOUT TO TAKE A BATH?
KNOCK FIRST.
YOU'RE THE ONE WHO NEVER KNOCKS.
HANG A TOWEL ON THE DOOR-KNOB.
SINCE THE LOCK IS STILL BROKEN.
KANAME KURAN...
I WONDER WHAT HE HAS IN MIND FOR YOU...

HUH?
...
...
NEVER MIND.
LEAVE ALREADY.
SHFF
WAIT.
DON'T GET SO CLOSE TO ME.
I FORGOT TO TELL YOU SOME-THING.
ZERO, YOU WERE JUST IMAGINING IT.

I'VE NEVER WANTED TO GIVE MY BLOOD TO KANAME.
IS THAT RIGHT?
YEAH... I JUST TOLD YOU.
YOU'RE THE ONE WHO BROUGHT IT UP.
SAYING WEIRD THINGS.
I HAVE THE RESPONSI-BILITY OF PROVIDING YOU WITH BLOOD.
THAT'S WHAT I INTEND TO DO FOREVER.
I CAN'T BE OVERLY GENEROUS AND GIVE OUT BLOOD WILLY-NILLY.
YOU MAY SEE ME AS A PUSHY DONOR, ZERO, BUT...
LOOK AT ME. ARE YOU LISTEN-ING?!
I HOPE YOU'RE NOT GOING TO SAY NO AGAIN.

WE...
...DECIDED TOGETHER, RIGHT?
BOTH OF US.
HUH?
THOK
GRIP
OUCH!

NOW?
JOLT

YOU FOOL.
YOU'RE THE ONE WHO HASN'T BEEN ABLE TO MAKE UP YOUR MIND.
GET OUT.
TOOF

I THOUGHT YOU WERE SERIOUS!
YOU JERK!
...
FLUP
GRAB
I'LL BE REALLY ANGRY...
...IF YOU TEST ME AGAIN!
SLAM
CHAK
WHAT, WHAT? YUKI LOOKS ANGRY.
...

BUT SINCE WE'RE BOTH HERE, KIRYU...
SHFF
I NEED TO TALK TO YOU.
PRIVATELY.
WHAT IS IT?
THE HUNTERS SOCIETY, A SECRET GOVERNMENT AGENCY...
...IS ASKING FOR YOU SPECIFICALLY...
...TO HUNT DOWN A LEVEL E SERIAL KILLER.
IT'S A WRITTEN DIRECTIVE.
OH DEAR... THEY INTEND TO TEST YOU TO SEE IF YOU'RE FIT FOR SERVICE.
I JUST TOLD THEM THE OTHER DAY THAT YOU'RE DOING FINE.
I...
I'M SORRY ABOUT THIS, ZERO...

...BUT YOU CANNOT REFUSE.
PEEK
THERE HE GOES.
I WONDER WHERE HE'S OFF TO? HE'S CUTTING HIS AFTERNOON CLASSES!
OH
COULD HE BE RUNNING AWAY?!
HUH?
HE WOULDN'T RUN AWAY NOW.
BUT WHAT IF...
LAST NIGHT...

DID I SAY...
...SOME-THING WRONG?
BUT WHAT I SAID...
...IS ALL I CAN MANAGE TO SAY RIGHT NOW...
...ABOUT ZERO AND ME...
...AND KANAME...

● Theme No. 2 "In the Style of a Dating Sim Game for Girls" (smile). This arose from deluded talks with my editor.

Who's the easiest to conquer?

We reached the conclusion that if you do it right, Aido and Shiki are easy to get. That's because they're not as warped inside as the other characters. And the fantasies continue on... (smile) (I'm sorry.♪)

With Kain and Ichijo, you can become friends, but it will be hard for the friend ship to develop into love. The problem is probably that it's difficult to read their inner thoughts. Kain moves to his own rhythm, and Ichijo's smile is an impregnable fortress...

Then there are Zero and Kaname... It would be better not to delve any deeper.

I would like to try conquering Yuki.

HEH
COME ON. DON'T ASK QUESTIONS--SHOOT FIRST.
OR ELSE I CAN...
...SLASH HER NECK BEFORE YOU PULL THE TRIGGER.
MAYBE THIS IS YOUR FIRST HUNT?
YOU'RE SUCH A KIND HUNTER.
RIN
BAM
HAHAHAHAHA!
YOU CAN'T SACRIFICE THE HOSTAGE, NOR CAN YOU SAVE HER. I FEEL SORRY FOR YOU.
HAHAHAHAHA!
KRRUK

THOOM
HA.
HA
HA
HA.
WHY ARE
VAMPIRES
LIKE THIS?
I SHOULD
HAVE
KNOWN.
HA
HA.
THEY DON'T
DESERVE ANY
SYMPATHY.
I'LL...
...END
IT ALL.

THIS...
...IS THE PLACE.
SHIKI, YOU'LL GET A SUNBURN WITHOUT A PARASOL.
OH!
RIMA.
SHIKI.
I'LL BE WAITING FOR YOU OVER THERE.
FINISH YOUR ERRAND QUICKLY OR YOU'LL BE LATE FOR THE PHOTO SHOOT!
AND SHIKI, YOU GET SUNBURNT EASILY, SO YOU GET UNDER RIMA'S PARASOL TOO!
YOU'RE A PROFESSIONAL MODEL!
WHY MINE?
OKAY.

WHY DO WE HAVE TO HUNT A FORMER HUMAN DURING THE DAY?
IT'S AN ORDER FROM THE SENATE. THEY DON'T WANT THE SOCIETY TO HUNT IT DOWN FIRST.
EH? WE'RE COMPETING WITH THEM?
OUR TARGET BECAME A LEVEL E ONLY RECENTLY, SO IT COULD STILL BE QUITE INTEL-LIGENT.
THAT WON'T MAKE MUCH OF A DIFFERENCE THOUGH.
OH?
IT'S THE DISCIPLINARY COMMITTEE GIRL.
OH!
SHIKI AND TOYA.
UM...
WHY ARE YOU NIGHT CLASS STUDENTS HERE?
PLIK

LOOK.
MY COMRADES CAME TO SEE ME?
SORRY, BUT I'M BUSY NOW.
DO YOU INTEND TO SWIPE MY DESSERT?
THAT'S NOT FAIR.
A VAMPIRE!
I CAN'T LET YOU DO THAT.
I'M SAVING HER FOR LATER.
TUMP
KA TAH
Y...
YOU INTEND TO FIGHT?!
VEER

SHOVE
GET OUT OF THE WAY.
RIIV
FWIK
BAM BAM
BAM

HUH? IT RAN AWAY.
WHY ARE YOU JUST STANDING AROUND? HURRY!
VISH
I DON'T LIKE CHASING...
GO AFTER IT!
DASH
HEY!
ZERO MUST BE IN THE ABANDONED HOUSE.
HE WENT AFTER THAT LEVEL E?!
GRIP

GOOD AFTER-NOON.
...
I'M LUCKY.
YOU'RE THE SECOND GIRL TODAY.
TUG
WMP
AHH!
COME HERE. I'LL BE NICE.
CLENCH

BLAM
BLAM
!
VISH
YOUR STUPID GAME OF TAG IS FINALLY OVER.
VUP

TOOM

CHIK
CROSSING
DON'T YOU DARE TOUCH HER...
...WITH YOUR FILTHY HANDS.
THIS IS THE END.

ZERO, WHAT'S GOING ON?
TMP
YUKI!
DON'T TRY TO STOP ME.
I'M UNDER ORDERS.
YOUR DESIRE FOR BLOOD HAS TURNED YOU INTO A SERIAL KILLER.
I WILL PURGE YOU OF YOUR SIN.
OH DEAR...
I'VE BEEN CAUGHT.

BUT NOW I WON'T HAVE TO KILL ANYMORE, RIGHT?

BLAM

KLAK
...
HEY, DISCIPLINARY COMMITTEE.
WE FOUND A GIRL OVER HERE. WHAT SHOULD WE DO?
SHE'S STILL ALIVE.

THAT'S GREAT, ZERO.
THE GIRL IS STILL ALIVE.
THANK YOU...
...FOR RESCUING ME TOO.
YOU WILL NOT DOUBLE-CROSS HER.

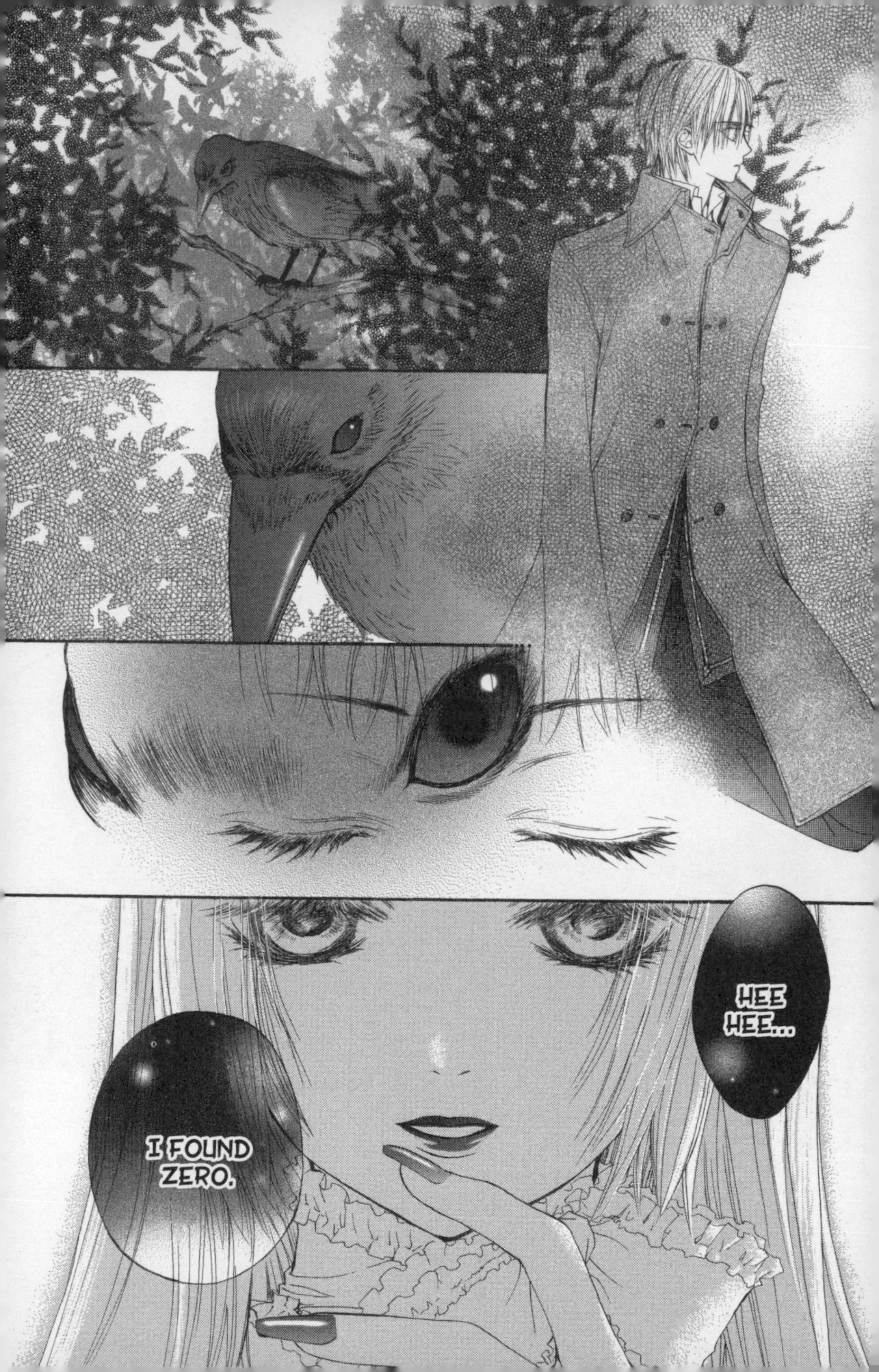
HEE HEE...
I FOUND ZERO.

OOOOH.
HIS EYES ARE SO SAD. HOW WONDERFUL! ♡
I'M SO GLAD HE'S BECOME SUCH A DISHY BOY. ♡♡
KICK
KICK
AND...
...HE HAS SUCH A DELICIOUS-LOOKING CHILD WITH HIM.
LICK
FWAP
YES.
I'LL ATTEND CROSS ACADEMY TOO.
THIRTEENTH NIGHT/END

VAMPIRE KNIGHT

FOURTEENTH NIGHT: THE LATE ARRIVAL: A NEW STUDENT

PLEASE!
TMP TMP
DAY CLASS STUDENTS CAN'T GO BEYOND THIS POINT AT THIS HOUR.
LET US GET A LITTLE CLOSER!
STEALTH
TUP

DOIK
IF YOU TRY TO TAKE EVEN ONE STEP FORWARD...
...I'LL MAKE YOU CRY.
DON'T WORRY! GO FOR IT!
BE BRAVE!
KIRYU ISN'T AS SCARY NOWADAYS. JUST DO IT!
KIRYU, YOU SUCK FOR THREATENING A GIRL!
HEY...
TUP
YEAH! YEAH!
AN INVISIBLE BORDER
YOU SHOULDN'T GIVE ME SO MUCH TROUBLE...
KYAH!
KYAH!
STOMP

WAIT!
SWARM
YOU REALLY CAN'T COME ANY CLOSER!
SUFF
!
PUSH
PUSH
I ONLY WANT TO TAKE ONE PHOTO!
NO...
STOP!
PUSH
SHALL I HELP CONTROL THEM FOR YOU?
JUST KIDDING.
KREEE
TUG
HUH?

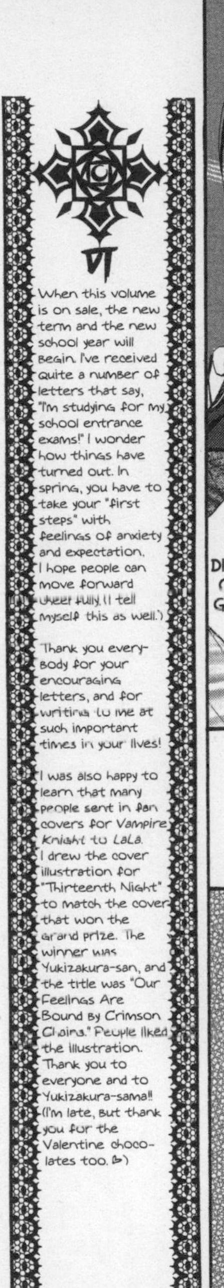
When this volume is on sale, the new term and the new school year will begin. I've received quite a number of letters that say, "I'm studying for my school entrance exams!" I wonder how things have turned out. In spring, you have to take your "first steps" with feelings of anxiety and expectation. I hope people can move forward cheerfully. (I tell myself this as well.)
Thank you everybody for your encouraging letters, and for writing to me at such important times in your lives!
I was also happy to learn that many people sent in fan covers for Vampire Knight to LaLa. I drew the cover illustration for "Thirteenth Night" to match the cover that won the grand prize. The winner was Yukizakura-san, and the title was "Our Feelings Are Bound by Crimson Chains." People liked the illustration. Thank you to everyone and to Yukizakura-sama!! (I'm late, but thank you for the Valentine chocolates too.)

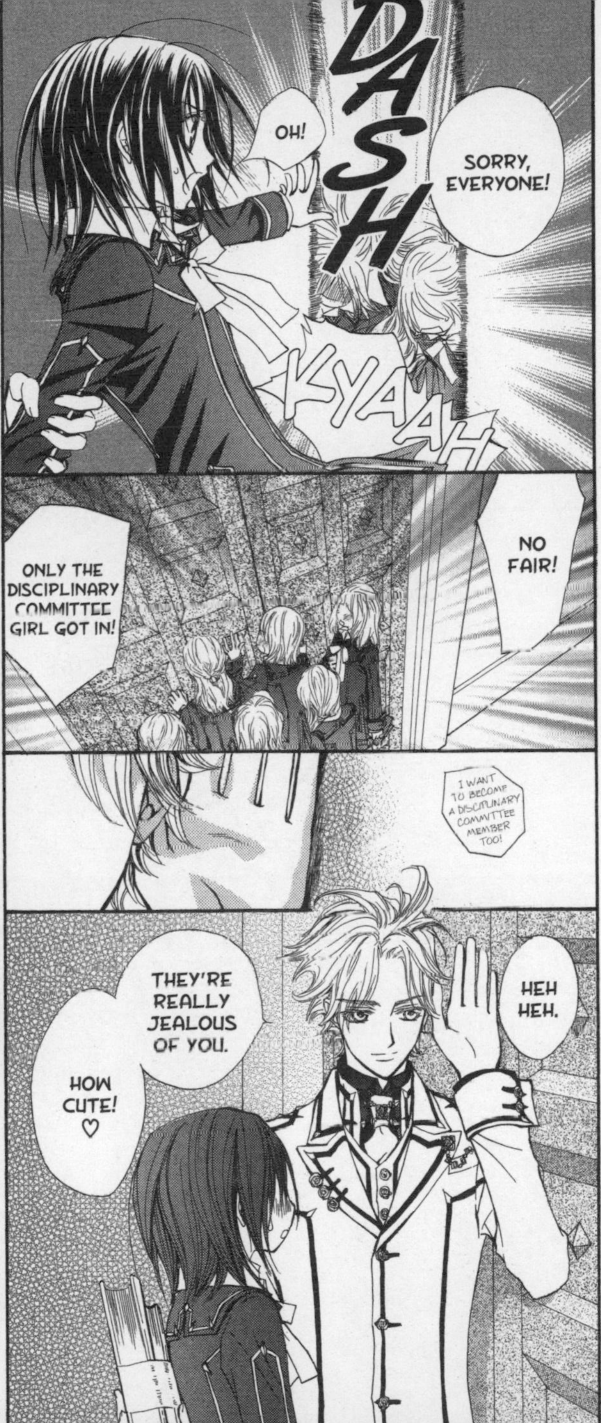
DASH
SORRY, EVERYONE!
OH!
KYAAAH
NO FAIR!
ONLY THE DISCIPLINARY COMMITTEE GIRL GOT IN!
I WANT TO BECOME A DISCIPLINARY COMMITTEE MEMBER TOO!
HEH HEH.
THEY'RE REALLY JEALOUS OF YOU.
HOW CUTE! ♡

UM...
WOULD YOU LET ME GO?
I HAVE TO GET BACK.
TMP
TMP
YOU ACT THAT WAY AFTER I JUST RESCUED YOU?!
AIDO, YOU'RE MAKING IT DIFFICULT FOR THE DISCIPLINARY COMMITTEE MEMBER...
!
YUKI...
...DON'T TAKE YOUR DUTIES SO FAR THAT YOU END UP GETTING HURT.
HMPH
UM.
KANAME...
YES.
I'LL BE CAREFUL.
BUT IF I LET OTHERS RESCUE ME, I'M OF NO USE AS A DISCIPLINARY COMMITTEE MEMBER...
I MEAN...
CHAK

GRAB
WHY DID YOU LET YOUR-SELF BE CARRIED OFF?
COME ON.

TAK
ARE YOU ANGRY THAT I LET ZERO GO ON THAT ASSIGNMENT, YUKI?
ZERO WAS BORN A HUNTER, SO ANOTHER ASSIGNMENT WOULD HAVE EVENTUALLY COME TO HIM.
ARE YOU SAYING IT'S HIS DUTY?
IN ORDER FOR ZERO TO LIVE AS A HUMAN, YES.
...
BY THE WAY, THERE'S SOME-THING I'D LIKE TO ASK YOU, YUKI.
I WANT YOU TO SHOW A NEW TRANSFER STUDENT AROUND.
A NEW...
...TRANSFER STUDENT?

YES... SHE WAS SUPPOSED TO ENROLL EARLIER...
...BUT SHE HAS BEEN RECUPERATING FROM AN ILLNESS IN A MOUNTAIN VILLA.
SHFF
KNOK KNOK
AH, I GUESS SHE'S HERE.
COME IN.
CHAK
UM...
GOOD EVENING.
WHAT?!
A NIGHT CLASS STUDENT?!

THIS IS...
...MARIA KURENAI.
ALLOW ME TO PRESENT MY DAUGHTER, YUKI.
NICE TO MEET YOU.
...
SHE LOOKS DELICIOUS... SO HEALTHY...
HEY!
YOU MUSTN'T SAY THINGS LIKE THAT IN THIS ACADEMY!
OOPS!
SMILE
I'M SORRY.
NICE TO MEET YOU, YUKI.
SMILE
CAN'T HELP BUT SMILE BACK

...
THE SCHOOL LIBRARY IS OVER THAT WAY, BUT IT'S CLOSED AT THIS HOUR...
...SO THE NIGHT CLASS STUDENTS USE THE DORMITORY LIBRARY.
UM...
THIS IS THE ROOM THE NIGHT CLASS IS USING TODAY.
HALT
WHAT'S WRONG?
...
YUKI.
WILL YOU BELIEVE ME IF I TELL YOU I'M SCARED OF TRANSFERRING HERE?
EVERYONE WILL PROBABLY IGNORE A FRAIL VAMPIRE LIKE ME.
SEE! YOU DON'T BELIEVE ME!
NO...
I WAS JUST A BIT SURPRISED.
BUT I THINK YOU'LL BE OKAY.
THE PRESIDENT AND THE VICE PRESIDENT ARE BOTH KIND.
IN ANY CASE...

...YOU CAN ALWAYS COME TO ME OR THE HEAD-MASTER.
WE'LL DO WHAT WE CAN.
DON'T WORRY, MARIA.
GLOMP
THANK YOU.
I REALLY LIKE GIRLS LIKE YOU...

THERE'S A LATE ARRIVAL... A TRANSFER STUDENT.
ARE YOU TALKING ABOUT THE BOOK YOU'RE READING?
HOW MYSTERIOUS... SOMETHING ISN'T RIGHT.
NO. A TRANSFER STUDENT IS REALLY COMING HERE.
CHMF
CHMF
NOOOOO!
MY POKKIN CHOCO! I WANTED TO GIVE SOME TO DORM PRESIDENT KURAN!
TODAY ISN'T GOING WELL AT ALL...
HEE HEE
HEE HEE
HEE HEE
HEE HEE

HEE HEE
THIS LOOKS LIKE A FUN GROUP! ♡
WHAT? CLASS HASN'T STARTED YET?
WHO THE HELL...
...ARE YOU?
"WHO THE HELL"?
VISH
VUP

HEY, BOY...
TMP
YOU THINK YOU CAN TALK THAT WAY TO ME?
JOLT
YOU SHOULD INTRODUCE YOURSELF FIRST...
...MARIA KURENAI.
OH...

I'M SORRY I UPSET YOU...
TOUCH
KANAME ...
...SAMA.
OOH!
MARIA IS SO HAPPY THAT SHE'S MET A PUREBLOOD!
...
WHAT?!
HOW DO YOU DO.

HMM.
FORGIVE ME. I THINK...
...I'VE RUINED THE ATMOSPHERE.
HEE HEE
I THINK IT'S BEST IF I LEAVE RIGHT NOW.
TMP

ZERO.
...
GRMP
TMP
YUKI?
VOOSH
PUM
YOU'RE LOAFING OFF, ZERO!
OW! WHY ARE YOU SUDDENLY--

THE HEAD-MASTER TOLD ME ALL ABOUT IT.
THE GIRL YOU SAVED, ZERO.
HER MEMORY WAS ERASED, AND SHE'S DOING FINE NOW.
SO YOU DON'T HAVE TO WORRY, RIGHT?
NO.
I DIDN'T HUNT THAT LEVEL E IN ORDER TO HELP SOMEONE.
MY WILL HAD NOTHING TO DO WITH IT.
IT'S SIMPLY WORK.
A VAMPIRE HUNTER'S DUTY...
IF THAT'S WHAT YOU'RE TELLING ME...
...THAT'S FINE. IF IT'S...
SUMP
...WHAT YOU'VE CONVINCED YOURSELF YOU'RE DOING.
BUT YOU NEVER LEARN FROM YOUR MISTAKES.
THAT'S WHY YOU WENT OFF ALONE, RIGHT?

IF YOU SUDDENLY LEAVE TO GO HUNT A VAMPIRE...
...WITHOUT TELLING ANYONE...
...WHO DO YOU THINK WOULD WORRY THE MOST?
I THOUGHT FOR A MOMENT THAT YOU HAD RUN AWAY...
HUH?
SO I FOLLOWED YOU, AND THINGS TURNED OUT THE WAY THEY DID.
SIGH
YOU KNOW...
I FEEL THAT SOME-DAY...
...YOU'LL GO OFF TO AVENGE YOUR FAMILY WITHOUT TELLING ME ANYTHING.
I'M NOT OBLIGATED TO TELL YOU ANYWAY.
YOU ARE.
GRIP

I'M THE ONE WHO IS GOING TO KILL YOU, RIGHT, ZERO?
THE GUN YOU GAVE ME FOR THAT DAY...
...IS IN MY DESK DRAWER.
I WON'T FORGET MY PROMISE.
YEAH... IF I JUST DISAPPEARED, YOU WOULDN'T BE ABLE TO KEEP YOUR PROMISE...
HEH
...AND YOU WOULDN'T KNOW WHAT TO DO.
BUT YOU'RE ASSUMING THAT I'LL BE BEATEN AT MY OWN GAME.
YOU DON'T HAVE MUCH FAITH, DO YOU?
HUH?

POOM
YOU'RE THE LAST PERSON WHO SHOULD BE TELLING ME THAT!
BUT I TRUST YOU...
...OKAY?
YOU...
KOFF
TAK

WHAT HAPPENED, MARIA?

I JOKED AROUND TOO MUCH...
...AND EVERYONE HATES ME NOW.
...
ZERO?
YOU...

NO!
!
HUFF
PULLING THAT GUN ON HER FOR NO REASON...!
WHY, ZERO?!

CHIK
YOU'RE WRONG.
WHO...
...IS SHE?
HOW DO YOU DO?
I'M MARIA KURENAI.

I'M SORRY HE SCARED YOU, MARIA.
HE'S A SCHOOL GUARDIAN LIKE I AM.
HE'S ZERO KIRYU, MY PARTNER.
HE DOESN'T USUALLY GO THIS FAR... WELL, ACTUALLY...
BUT I SHOULDN'T HAVE BEEN WANDERING AROUND THE GROUNDS.
I'M SORRY.
AND...
...THANK YOU FOR PROTECTING ME, YUKI.
YOU'RE A GOOD GIRL. I REALLY LIKE YOU.
I KNOW...
...GIRLS LIKE YOU TASTE REALLY DELICIOUS.

BE MY FRIEND.
MARIA KURENAI TRANSFERRED HERE OFFICIALLY AND TOOK THE VOW.
SHE WAS BORN FRAIL, AND HAS NEVER ATTENDED A NIGHT PARTY.
THAT'S ABOUT IT.
I DON'T FIND ANYTHING STRANGE ABOUT HER...
WELL...
...EXCEPT THAT SHE'S FEARLESS.
...
AKATSUKI.
HAVE YOU EVER SEEN THAT WOMAN?
WHAT WOMAN?

THE PUREBLOOD VAMPIRE WHO COMES FROM A LINEAGE ON PAR WITH KURAN...
SHE DISAP-PEARED AFTER GOING BERSERK.
HER NAME IS SHIZUKA HIO.
SHE DISAPPEARED AFTER THE KIRYU FAMILY INCIDENT.
SOME SAY SHE DIED AFTER THAT.
I'VE NEVER MET HER.
WHAT DID YOU WANT TO KNOW?
NO... IT'S NOTHING.
LET'S STOP TALKING ABOUT HER. IT'S UNLUCKY.

KANAME ...
WHAT'S TO BE DONE...
...WITH THAT TRANSFER STUDENT?
WELL, YOU CAN TAKE CARE OF HER, ICHIJO.
ME?!
IT'D BE A PROBLEM IF I DO ANYTHING IN THE OPEN.
AND THIS ACADEMY HAS ALL THE PIECES...
...THAT SHE WANTS...
TUP
"PIECES"... THAT'S A GOOD WAY OF PUTTING IT.
IS IT A COINCIDENCE?

NO.
I ARRANGED THINGS THIS WAY...
FOURTEENTH NIGHT/END

THE FATHER WHO RAISED ME IS THE HEADMASTER OF CROSS ACADEMY, A PRIVATE SCHOOL.
MY LIFE WAS SAVED...
...BY A KIND VAMPIRE...
VAMPIRE KNIGHT
SIDE STORY: THE WARMTH THAT SLIPPED FROM HER PALM. AND...
THIS HAPPENED BEFORE THE NIGHT CLASS WAS ESTABLISHED AT CROSS ACADEMY.

TUP
...
HEAD-MASTER?
PHOO
WHY NOT CALL HIM FATHER WHEN YOU'VE GOT A COLD?
B-BMP
KANAME-SAMA...
WHEN I OPENED MY EYES, THE PERSON I REALLY LIKED WAS THERE.

B-BMP
YOU'LL CATCH MY COLD...
HEH
I'LL BE ALL RIGHT.
YOU STILL HAVE A HIGH FEVER.
I'M SORRY FOR WAKING YOU.
SLEEP A LITTLE BIT MORE...
...YUKI.
NO.
IF I FALL ASLEEP, YOU'LL GO HOME, KANAME-SAMA.

ALL RIGHT.
IF YOU WON'T SLEEP, I'LL LEAVE.
NO...
NO!
I'LL SLEEP! PLEASE STAY WITH ME...
...BECAUSE WE DON'T GET TO BE TOGETHER VERY OFTEN.
THEN...
CLOSE YOUR EYES...
...AND DON'T MAKE ME WORRY...

WHEN I WAS TOLD YOU COLLAPSED WITH A HIGH FEVER, YUKI...
...MY HEART FROZE FOR A MOMENT.
REALLY?
EVEN THOUGH YOU SAY SO...
REALLY.
HOLD
...WHEN I OPEN MY EYES, I KNOW YOU WON'T BE HERE.
KANAME-SAMA...
I DON'T WANT YOU TO LEAVE...
...SO I'LL KEEP HOLDING YOUR HAND...

OH
SHUFF
GRIP

CHAK
ZERO?
WHAT'RE YOU DOING?

...
NOTHING.
...
PAT
TMP
THE FLOOR ...
...IT'S WARM...
THE WARMTH THAT SLIPPED FROM HER PALM. AND.../END

VAMPIRES COVERED IN BLOOD ARE PROHIBITED FROM ENTERING THIS PAGE!!

✿YUKI'S IMAGE OF ZERO IN HER MIND✿

To those who really get me in the mood to draw my manga, my readers.
To my editor, everybody in the LaLa department, and the other people involved.
I make them worry, and I inconvenience them.
To O. Mio-sama, K. Midori-sama, A. Ichika-sama, K. Yoshiru-sama,
and M. Kaoru-sama, who help me with my manuscripts.
To my mother and my friends. You are a great help.
To my grandmother, who watches over me tenderly.
I thank you all from the bottom of my heart!!

樋野まつり でした。
Hino Matsuri

The story will really move (←?。)
in vols. 4 and 5!!

EDITOR'S NOTES

Characters

Matsuri Hino puts careful thought into the names of her characters in *Vampire Knight*, so in each chapter of *Shojo Beat* magazine you'll find an explanation of the kanji for one character's name. Below is the collection of names that have run in *Shojo Beat* through volume 3. Each character's name is presented family name first, per the kanji reading.

黒主優姫

Cross Yuki

Yuki's last name, *Kurosu*, is the Japanese pronunciation of the English word "cross." However, the kanji has a different meaning—*kuro* means "black" and *su* means "master." Her first name is a combination of *yuu*, meaning "tender" or "kind," and *ki*, meaning "princess."

錐生零

Kiryu Zero

Zero's first name is the kanji for *rei*, meaning "zero." In his last name, *Kiryu*, the *ki* means "auger" or "drill," and the *ryu* means "life."

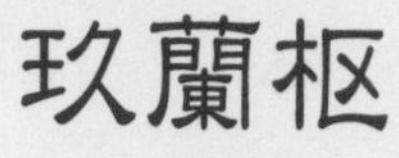

Kuran Kaname

Kaname means "hinge" or "door." The kanji for his last name is a combination of the old-fashioned way of writing *ku*, meaning "nine," and *ran*, meaning "orchid": "nine orchids."

Aido Hanabusa

Hanabusa means "petals of a flower." *Aido* means "indigo temple." In Japanese, the pronunciation of *Aido* is very close to the pronunciation of the English word *idol*.

架院暁

Kain Akatsuki

Akatsuki means "dawn," or "day-break." In *Kain, ka* is a base or support, while *in* denotes a building that has high fences around it, such as a temple or school.

早園瑠佳

Souen Ruka

In *Ruka*, the *ru* means "lapis lazuli" while the *ka* means "good-looking," or "beautiful." The *sou* in Ruka's surname, *Souen*, means "early," but this kanji also has an obscure meaning of "strong fragrance." The *en* means "garden."

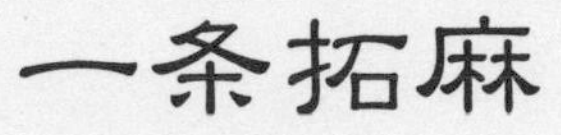

Ichijo Takuma

Ichijo can mean a "ray" or "streak." The kanji for *Takuma* is a combination of *taku*, meaning "to cultivate" and *ma*, which is the kanji for *asa*, meaning "hemp" or "flax," a plant with blue flowers.

Shiki Senri

Shiki's last name is a combination of *shi*, meaning "to support" and *ki*, meaning "mallow"—a flowering plant with pink or white blossoms. The *ri* in *Senri* is a traditional Japanese unit of measure for distance, and one *ri* is about 2.44 miles. Senri means "1,000 *ri*."

夜刈十牙

Yagari Toga

Yagari is a combination of *ya*, meaning "night," and *gari*, meaning "to harvest." *Toga* means "ten fangs."

一条麻遠, 一翁

Ichijo Asato, aka "Ichio"

Ichijo can mean a "ray" or "streak." Asato's first name is comprised of *asa*, meaning "hemp" or "flax," and *tou*, meaning "far off." His nickname is *ichi*, or "one," combined with *ou*, which can be used as an honorific when referring to an older man.

頼ちゃん

Yori-chan

Yori means "trust." In the Japanese version, Yuki uses the suffix "-chan" when referring to her best friend to show familiarity.

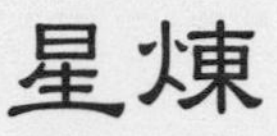

Seiren
Sei means "star" and *ren* means "to smelt" or "refine." *Ren* is also the same kanji used in *rengoku*, or "purgatory."

遠矢莉磨
Toya Rima
Toya means a "far-reaching arrow." Rima's given name is a combination of *ri*, or "jasmine," and *ma*, which signifies enhancement by wearing away, such as by polishing or scouring.

紅まり亜
Kurenai Maria
Kurenai means "crimson." The kanji for the last *a* in Maria's given name is the same that is used in "Asia."

Terms

pokyu: *Pokyu* is used to describe the sound of light, cute footsteps, like those of a child.

-sama: The suffix *sama* is used in formal address for someone who ranks higher in the social hierarchy. The vampires call their leader "Kaname-sama" only when they are among their own kind.

Matsuri Hino burst onto the manga scene with her series *Kono Yume ga Sameturu* (When This Dream Is Over), which was published in *LaLa DX* magazine. Hino was a manga artist a mere nine months after she decided to become one.

With the success of her popular series *Toraware no Minoue* (Captive Circumstance), and *MeruPuri*, Hino has established herself as a major player in the world of shojo manga. *Vampire Knight* is currently serialized in *LaLa* and *Shojo Beat* magazines.

Hino enjoys creative activities and has commented that she would have been either an architect or an apprentice to traditional Japanese craft masters if she had not become a manga artist.

VAMPIRE KNIGHT
Vol. 3
The Shojo Beat Manga Edition

This manga contains material that was originally published in English in *Shojo Beat* magazine, April 2007–August 2007 issues.

STORY AND ART BY
MATSURI HINO

Translation & English Adaptation/Tomo Kimura
Touch-up Art & Lettering/George Caltsoudas
Graphic Design/Nozomi Akashi
Editor/Nancy Thistlethwaite

Editor in Chief, Books/Alvin Lu
Editor in Chief, Magazines/Marc Weidenbaum
VP of Publishing Licensing/Rika Inouye
VP of Sales/Gonzalo Ferreyra
Sr. VP of Marketing/Liza Coppola
Publisher/Hyoe Narita

Printed in Canada

Published by VIZ Media, LLC
P.O. Box 77010
San Francisco, CA 94107

Shojo Beat Manga Edition
10 9 8 7 6 5 4 3 2 1
First printing, October 2007

PARENTAL ADVISORY
VAMPIRE KNIGHT is rated T+ for Older Teen and is recommended for ages 16 and up. This volume contains sexual themes and violence.
ratings.viz.com